The Business Goal Setting Guide

13 Easy Steps To Help You Set Goals And Achieve Lasting Success In Both Your Careers And Personal Life

The Business Goal Setting Guide

Table of Contents

Introduction: 3

Chapter 1 - Your Goal and How to Set It The SMART Way..4

Chapter 2 - Take A Journey Of Self Discovery...........9

Chapter 3 - Identify the Goals that can Bring the Most Benefits...12

Chapter 4 - See The Big Picture...............................17

Chapter 5 - Create A Goal Timeline..........................19

Chapter 6 - Make Sure Your Goals Are Positive.......21

Chapter 7 - Identify The Limiting Factors.................23

Chapter 8 - About Your Quarterly And Yearly Goals..26

Chapter 9 - Schedule Your Goals According To Priority..28

Chapter 10 - Set Small Incremental Goals...............30

Chapter 11 - Designing A Plan..................................32

Chapter 12 - Carry Out Your Plan And Track Your Progress...34

Chapter 13 - Review Your Goals And See If Something Is Amiss..36

Conclusion..38

Introduction

I want to thank you and congratulate you for purchasing the book, *"The Business Goal Setting Guide"*.

This book contains proven steps and strategies on how to set your goals, covered in 13 easy steps to help you live a fulfilling life that you deserve.

If you will just accept the things that come your way and go in the direction where the mighty wind takes you, then don't be surprised to find yourself in a situation and place that you may find unacceptable. Why did it happen? It's because you did not set your goals properly.

It only takes a fraction of your time each day to set your goals that will take you where you want to be in the future, and the effects can last a lifetime.

Thanks again for purchasing this book, I hope you enjoy it!

Chapter 1 - Your Goal and How to Set It The SMART Way

Life can be difficult to manage if you don't have goals. Some just literally go with the flow and go where the wind blows them. Such thinking is rather risky because what you do today has an impact on what you will achieve in the future.

If you want your life to have direction and lead to happiness and fulfillment, then you need to set your goals. It is not that difficult to do, but you will need a lot of patience, willpower, self-control, discipline, determination, diligence, and courage in order to pull it off. Getting started can make you feel overwhelmed, but you need to focus on the things that you will gain once you put everything in motion.

Setting goals gives you a sort of power to steer your life in a good direction to achieve success in whatever you choose. Understand that there are goals that demand a lifetime to attain, while there are other goals that you can easily accomplish within the day. Setting and realizing your goals can give you an undeniable feeling of satisfaction and your accomplishments will constantly remind you that you worked hard and deserve the feeling of success.

What is a Goal?

A goal is the outcome that you want to achieve; a desire, or a target life that you want to live. People have different grounds, purposes, and motivations for setting their goals. There are people who want to improve their quality of life, achieve a specific dream, live happily, or live for a long time.

Goal setting helps you decide how to live your life, turn a clear idea into a reality, and keep you focused. Research studies show that people who have goals are more productive, tend to be wealthier and successful, more fulfilled, and happy.

Setting your own feasible goals and following your plan of action in achieving them can help a lot in steering your life on the course that you intended to follow.

Where do you want your Life to lead you?

Some people are just too lazy to plan for theirs; that's why they choose to just go with the flow. Your desires and aspirations are different from anyone else's, although you may have similar desires and goals. You may desire wealth and power, financial success, a happy family life, a good business, fulfilling career, and a healthy relationship with someone you love. You can have anything that you want if you have set your goals clearly and follow your plan to achieve them.

You need to be careful, because a wrong goal can lead you to frustration, unhappiness, and potential downfall. To avoid setting wrong goals, you can follow the S-M-A-R-T way.

Planning your Goal the SMART Way

SMART stands for **S**pecific, **M**easurable, **A**ttainable, **R**elevant, and **T**ime-bound, which is usually used by life coaches, educators for goal identification systems, human resources departments, and motivators to make their audience or students remember the essential aspects of goal setting.

The secret to effectively set your goals is to create a clear definition of the things that you want to achieve. It is not enough to declare that you want to be famous, powerful, or wealthy. You are declaring something vague, which does not clearly say anything about when you expect to achieve it and how. It is not even clear what kind of fame you are after, the strength you wish to have, or fortune that you want to gain. It is impossible to design a specific action plan if your desires are too vague. You need to write down the things that you desire, the SMART way.

Make sure that you have Specific Goals

You need to determine what you are dying to accomplish, when you plan to do it, where will you do it, why must you do it, and who the people involved are. You can briefly say how you plan to accomplish your goal and just elaborate on the details when you begin creating your complete plan in accomplishing your objective.

Instead of just saying, "I want to be slim," say "I will attend an aerobic class every Friday near our office with some friends and get the figure I want in two months' time." You will also be compelled to follow your own schedule because you set it yourself. You need to keep in mind that you need feasible goals.

Make your Goal Measurable

It is important that your goals are measurable. You will be able to see your milestones and track your progress along the way, which can motivate you even more as you come close to the realization of you goal. Saying, "I am going to jog more" is difficult to measure and keep track of your progress. But, if you say, "I am going to jog around the block 10 times" it is easy to measure how you are doing since you have a specific number of rounds that you plan to take.

Measureable goals can also help you to see if you are really moving towards your goals. It usually answers the question how; such as how many, how much, how thick, how swift, and so on.

Your Goals Must be Attainable

When setting your goals, it is important to evaluate your situation and capability with all honesty so that you will be able to set realistic and feasible goals. Avoid something far-fetched and anything that seems impossible to attain no matter how hard you try. Aim for something that you can do within your current capabilities to avoid frustration. If you are able to take your abilities to the next level and you are confident that you can reach your initial goal without getting depressed, then proceed as you wish.

Target Relevant Goals

Relevant goals must be focused on the things that you want in your life. They are in direct contrast with scattered or conflicting goals. The goals you set must be in harmony with everything that you consider significant in your life, from your success in your endeavors, to your happiness that you can share with the people close to your heart.

Your Goals must be Time-bound

You should not just set a goal and then do nothing while waiting for it to happen. You might wait forever if you do that and it is not even right to call it goal setting, because you are merely wishing for it to happen as you wait for a miracle.

You should make your goals time-bound so that have specific due dates. You should aim to accomplish your goals on or before the due date that you have set. In setting deadlines, you need to carefully determine the right amount of time that you will need to accomplish a particular goal without putting too much pressure on yourself, but not to make you feel too carefree.

Once you have determined the goals that you want to achieve, use the SMART way of setting them and try to achieve them in the least possible time.

Chapter 2 - Take A Journey Of Self Discovery

You need to discover your real self first in order to set your goal straight. Self discovery is a life changing journey that you need to consider in order to appreciate the purpose of your existence. You might even be questioning the purpose or significance of your existence right now.

Who you really are and whether or not you are needed. You might even wonder why you were born, if you can do something to make the world better, do you deserve to enjoy life, what kind of existence will you have in case you were not born as you are, or will you be able to do better than any scientists? Is there a precise answer to all of these questions?

There are still so many things that you need to know about yourself and you still need to find the true extent of your capabilities, and you can only find them if you take a journey to discover your inner self.

The Journey to your Inner Self

To be able to clearly identify the goals that you need to set; you need to know your true self and discover the things that you are truly capable of. You need to be prepared to welcome the things that you will unfold in knowing your inner self. At first, you may not accept everything as the truth but you must in due time and that would be the moment when you can set the right goals for yourself.

You may feel lonely and empty because you might still be looking and reaching for things that won't give you absolute happiness such as fame and lots of money. In search of a number of things, you might forget to search for yourself.

When you take the road to self discovery, you will be dealing with things outside your comfort zone. The road could be bumpy but you will be thankful that you have decided to take it.

Think of the people that were, are, and will always be with you no matter what happens. Let the important people in your life know that you are on the verge of knowing your inner self. Find strength, support, and encouragement in their presence and words. Let them be your ray of light when darkness seems to engulf you.

You need courage, an open mind, and determination when taking this journey. Having a positive mindset can help you through any barrier that impedes you from realizing your full potential.

There are people who will try to bring you down, and there is always at least one person who will lift you up and that is enough. As long as there is someone who believes in you, that should be enough to try your best until the end. Take the hurtful words as challenge and get back at your detractors with all your might. You can teach your brain to filter out harsh words that can discourage you and get on with your life the way you should.

Balancing the Good and Evil Inside you

As you discover your inner self, you will face the good and evil within you. All people have a good and bad side, and you need to balance both in order to live peacefully. There are people who prefer or let their evil side to dominate while the good one sleeps for a while. Some choose to let the good one takes over but that does not prevent the evil one from trying to surface.

Your bad and good personality must be balanced. You should not let your good side rule all the time especially if you need to deal with someone who has a bad personality. On the other hand, letting your bad personality rule all the time can weaken your spirit and makes it impossible for you to meet your goal.

Discovering your inner self will make it easier for you to create a balance between your good and evil side and set free your full potential. You will be able to stir your life to the direction that you want to follow. You will be able to establish good rapport with other people, cultivate meaningful relationships, and live a happy and peaceful life.

Chapter 3 - Identify the Goals that can Bring the Most Benefits

Once you have learned who you really are and the things that you can do, then you will be able to identify the goals that you need to have in order to live a happy life together with your loved ones. You need to write them all and then group together the ones that you need to fulfill within a short span of time, in three months, or in a year.

A psychology professor found that people who list down their goals, share them with their trusted person, and gives weekly updates regarding their progress are 33% more successful than those who just keep their goals in their heads.

Identifying the goals you want to achieve (the SMART way) is just the start of setting your goal. You will still need to do some other things to make sure that you will achieve success in your career and personal life by setting the right goals to target.

Different Methods of Recording your Goals

Since study revealed that writing down your goals is more effective than keeping them in your head, we will discuss the two ways of recording your goals via writing.

Pen and Paper Method

The first one is using pen and paper. When you record your goals, it is best to choose a time and place where you can be alone and give your full attention to what you are doing. Remember that you are dealing with your life here and you need to make sure that your goals will be able to give you a life that you deserve.

It is advisable to jot everything in a journal or notebook to keep the pages intact – nothing will get lost.

Via Computer

If you are unfortunate enough to have a handwriting that is hard to read (even you find it hard to do so at times), then you can choose to store your data in your computer. Make sure to have a back up file in case something went wrong with your unit.

The beauty about using a computer is that you can have a beautiful lay out and it is easier to encode than write. The disadvantage, however, is that you won't be able to access your journal right away unlike the notebook which you only need to flip the page.

There are also apps that you can use so that you can access your entry via mobile phone, tablet, or your laptop or desktop. This way, you won't have any hard time accessing your files anytime and anywhere.

Assembling your Goals Book

To give you an idea on how to organize your goals, you need to group them according to their deadlines (see chapter 5 for the details). As mentioned earlier, you need to group the goals with the same time range together for easy monitoring. But first, you need to make some entries for the different areas in your life such as health, relationship, spirituality, finances, business, community, and leisure.

You need to take ample time to reflect on everything and determine the life that you want to lead by targeting the goals that you set.

Your Goals for Health

Your health is the most important area in your life. Your money won't be of much help if your health continues to fail. You need to set a goal of having a fit and healthy body all the time.

You may include the diet that you need to take, workout, healthy lifestyle to keep, bad habits to avoid, regular doctor visits, and other things that can help you achieve a healthy body. Avoid eating junk foods, sugar, and processed foods as much as possible.

Your Goals for Relationship

Your loved ones are the most important people in your life and you need to keep it that way. Maintain a healthy relationships with them especially your significant other. Set goals that will minimize misunderstandings and improve communications. You can also include spending quality time, discussing family matters, and other things that will help you keep a harmonious relationship with the people you love.

Your Goals for Spirituality

Having and maintaining a healthy spiritual life should be your goal to keep every aspect in your life balanced. Spirituality includes meditation, yoga, saying a prayer, rendezvous with nature, and other activities that can help you achieve peace of mind.

Your Goals for Finances

Setting your goals for your finances include savings for your retirement, becoming debt-free, fund for your kids' education, down payment for a home, improvements in your property, and anything else that can secure your future and that of your loved ones. You may also consider investing if the investment looks promising.

Your Goals for Business

Having your own business can somehow provide ease and security in the future. You need to set important goals for your business to make it flourish whether you already have your own or you are yet to establish one. Your goals may include ways to make your clients and employees satisfied and happy, increase productivity, provide good service, business expansion, make your business more profitable without diminishing the quality of your products and service, and other business related matters.

Your Goals for Community

Harmonious relations are important especially within the community. Being a volunteer and doing some other things that will benefit your entire community can give a different sense of fulfillment. It can also boost your self esteem and encourage personal growth.

You can make donations (cash and in kind), participate in community projects or organize one, become a volunteer, and anything that you can do for your community to get better.

Your Goals for Leisure

There are times when you need to be alone and continue to get in touch with your inner self, and take a break from work once in a while. You can also make it your goal to spend a nice vacation with your family to make your bond stronger. Some of the leisure activities that you can consider, aside form taking a vacation or travelling, are learning new crafts such as crocheting and knitting, dancing, painting, and other fun and worthwhile activities.

After listing your goals and reviewing if they are specific, measurable, attainable, and relevant, it is time to set the time frame to make your goals real SMART.

Chapter 4 - See The Big Picture

Take a look at the goals that you have written and see if there are "big picture" that you can break into smaller ones. This is usually applicable for goals that are considered medium or long-term. It is easier to achieve a goal if it's smaller and more precise.

If you want recognition, career wise, you may want to ask yourself what line of work do you consider ideal? What are the things that you need to do in order to get your dream job? What are the possible hindrances that prevent you from acquiring that job? Does the job require a specific training or education? Within these questions, there are possible smaller goals that you need to do first in order to succeed in your chosen career.

In terms of financial goals you may want to consider the amount of money that you need to acquire to live comfortably. It is also important to consider the source of your income. In order to gain financial freedom you might want to consider investing or putting up a business – you need to break either choice into smaller goals. If the scope of the goal seems too big, break it into smaller ones and concentrate from there until you have satisfied the bigger goal.

For your romantic relationship, you need to be clear about the kind of relationship that you want to foster – open relationship, long-term partner, marriage, or whatever option you both agreed to. What are the qualities you are looking for in a potential mate? You might need to have a lot of options in case your potential partner failed to meet some of the requirements but you want him or her anyway.

In raising a family you need to consider when to have your own children, are you up for adoption, or are you fine with having step children? In every marriage, the couple wants to have a child of their own, but what if your spouse has no ability to give you one? There are unexpected things that might come along and you can make adjustments or totally change your initial goal if you must.

The idea here is that if you think that a certain goal seems to be big, break it down and start working on the smaller goals until you have able to satisfy the bigger goal.

Chapter 5 - Create A Goal Timeline

Now that you have your goals, you need to review them and determine the timeframe for each goal that you have listed. Remember the SMART way of setting your goals? You need to have a specific time in achieving each goal and avoid a devil-may-care attitude. Setting a goal is useless if you don't have any concrete plan in achieving them.

Your goal timeline is similar to a life timeline. Instead of writing down the things that happened to you on certain dates, you write the things that you intend to achieve on or before the specified date arrives.

You need to be careful in assigning a specific time range for each goal and don't assign a random time period. It is best to determine first which goal should come first. Be careful in arranging your goals because there might be goals that you need to accomplish first before you can do the other one.

Make sure that your timeframes are realistic, feasible, and won't cause unnecessary worry on your part. There are times when failure to meet the deadline can frustrate and depress you. You set goals to bring ease and comfort in your life and not add difficulties.

Group the goals that you need to accomplish immediately, within three months, in a year, or other time range that you have set for your different goals. There are times when you need to make alterations in your timeframe because you made some modifications in your goals.

As you discover your inner self, some skills will suddenly surface which you never thought you had in you. There are times when you develop a new talent, which can help you realize a certain goal at a shorter time period.

You need to brace yourself and expect some sudden changes in you. As you improve, you also need to make some adjustments in your goals or your time frame or both.

Chapter 6 - Make Sure Your Goals Are Positive

In setting your goal, make sure to use positive statements to get you fired up. Positive statements are affirmations that you are making a commitment in achieving your goals.

In designing the plan that will take you to your goal, always say, "I will do this" or "I am going to finish that". Negative statements such as "I will not let anything to stop me" and "I will not allow pressure get the best of me" are already negating something although they both sound so bold.

Statements like "I will reach my goal according to my plan" and "I will remain calm and compose as I get near my goal" sound more assertive and determined.

Although the mentioned negative statements seem so bold, there is a hint of doubt. Saying such statements only mean that you have fears that something might stop you on your way to achieving your goals. You also fear that pressure will get to you eventually. The positive statements have more direction and you fear nothing to stop you. You will definitely reach your goal as planned and you will remain calm and compose because nothing will go wrong as you go near your goals.

Positive statements can drive you to move in positive ways – decisive, straight to the point, precise, and prompt. You will gather the right information and apply the right strategy in achieving you goals. You are sure of yourself, and you are certain about your actions. You spare no room for hesitations and always confident.

When you always say and do positive things, your actions somehow adapt your way of thinking and move in the same manner. You will act positively because you gave positive input. Unlike negative statements that can create confusion and hesitation. Although worrying might make you think of an alternative plan immediately in case the original plan fails, it will still bring more harm than good. If you are sure about the success of your plan, then having an alternative plan is just a waste of time and effort.

In achieving your goals, you need to employ everything in your power to achieve your objective within your capability. Remember to keep everything positive and the result will have the same effect.

Chapter 7 - Identify The Limiting Factors

Expect some obstacles in achieving your goal. Even though you have positive statements for your goals, there are still stubborn hindrances that will try to stop you from reaching your goal. If you are not careful in identifying the limiting factors, then you might eat a lot of time before you realize your goals.

For example, if your goal is to lose two pounds in a week by going to a local gym to do aerobics everyday for an hour after office hours, then you should be able to achieve such feat after seven days. If you failed to meet your goal despite the preciseness that involves in achieving it, then you did not properly identify the things that prevented you from meeting your goal.

Could it be that you were not able to keep your schedule to go there everyday? What were the things that prevented you from going to the gym? Were you too tired, you need to prepare the family dinner, you need someone to look after your child, or you can't say no to a friend who asked you to do something for her? Whatever reason you may have, you failed to meet your goal because you did not identify the possible obstacles that may come as you try to accomplish your goal.

Given the said scenario, you could've have adjusted your time to sleep and wake up early to make sure that you will be able to finish your work in time. You could have prepared the dinner in the morning before you go to work, put it in the refrigerator, and just heat it when dinnertime comes. Before starting your plan, you should've contacted someone to look after your child for an hour or two while you are in the gym. You should've informed your friends about your plan, that way you won't feel awkward when you refuse to do them a favor.

You can prevent getting face to face with the limiting factors if you have identified them in the first place and made necessary adjustments before proceeding with your plan. In every goal that you have written down, you need to know and identify if there are any hindrances that might prevent you from reaching your goal.

Things to Watch Out for

Your goals must be in harmony with your long-term plans and make sure that they are of utmost importance. If you have conflicting goals, then don't expect to attain success. The conflicts between your goals are preventing you from advancing. It is the reason why it is significant to have relevant goals.

When you have negative statements in writing your goals, you unconsciously develop fear of failure or self-doubt. You tend to put off your plan for another day and even lose your confidence as time goes by. If you have positive statements, you are more assertive and courageous in facing anything and nothing will be able to stop you from marching forward and grabbing your success.

Expect other external factors to prevent you in meeting your goal. You just need to focus on the problem at hand and find the root cause. You may need to make slight modifications in your goal or eliminate the cause on the spot.

Keep a positive mindset and open mind and you will be able to see the obstacles ahead and find appropriate solutions before you come face to face with them or deal with them head on with full intention of winning.

Chapter 8 - About Your Quarterly And Yearly Goals

Your quarterly and yearly goals are considered long-term goals and they are always shifting. The things that you view as urgent today may not have the same urgency next week, next month, or next year. It is advisable to break your yearly goals into quarterly goals to make it easier. However, there might be some yearly goals that might be impossible to break.

Keeping in touch with your inner self can help you polish yourself even more. There is a possibility that you will be able to achieve something within three months which is originally a yearly goal. It is important to update your goal list as you hone your skills and discover fresh ones. Self-discovery can help you a lot in making yourself better with each passing day.

Procrastination is your greatest enemy in long-term goals. Because it will take time before you see a milestone in your long-term goals, you might get tired of waiting and might even think that you are not making any progress at all. It is important to break the long-term goals into smaller ones before you even feel like you are getting tired of waiting. For the seemingly unbreakable ones, you just have to do your best in keeping your positivity all the time. You can always get back to them and find ways to break them into smaller ones especially if you have developed the skill you need to make them easier to deal with.

Your quarterly and yearly goals are just the same as your immediate goals and the only difference is the time of achieving them. You should record every bit of progress or milestone that you have for your long-term goals to avoid losing interest in pursuing them.

If you will follow your plan and just continue to improve yourself and make some modifications in your goals as you improve, then you will be able to see your goals coming true in a matter of time.

Chapter 9 - Schedule Your Goals According To Priority

When you put a time period for each goal, you need to properly determine which goal should come first. You need to be clear on when you plan to do it or if there is something that should be done first before you can proceed.

Immediate goals should be flexible to avoid hindrances. If you plan to do your exercise routine everyday at 4 a.m. for 30 minutes (no one is still up to bother you) and something suddenly pops up, you can postponed it for later but make sure not to forget. You can mark your calendar or planner to remind yourself. Sometimes there are sudden hindrances that you need to attend to immediately, but it should not keep you from accomplishing your goal for the day.

You need to focus on which goal should have your first priority. Keep in mind that there are goals that might not look like as urgent as the others, but you might need to do them first in order to make the more urgent goal easier to accomplish.

There are also times when you need to switch the priorities when you discover that you can still improve your goals. Making some modifications in your goal are acceptable as long as your goals are set the SMART way. Avoid contradicting goals at all cost because they can bring you more problems than you think. Instead of making your life easier, they might cause a disaster.

Time is of the essence when setting your goal. You need to spend lots of time in listing them down, determining their period, and other important factors. Remember that you are trying to stir your life to the direction, which you think is the perfect course to take.

Chapter 10 - Set Small Incremental Goals

Incremental goals are goals that you can easily complete in a day or a week. It is advisable to keep your incremental goals small especially if you need to see a milestone or you always monitor your progress.

You can break your long-term goals into small incremental goals to see your milestones and prevent your motivation from depleting while completing your long-term goal. If your goal is to be able to play at least three musical instruments in two years, then you can break that long-term goal to learn one instrument every eight months.

To learn a musical instrument, you need to practice at least five days in a week. The amount of practice might be too much for you at first, you need to turn it into incremental goals to make sure that you will be able to learn that particular instrument in eight months.

You can start practicing for two days in a week for at least one month, three days in a week in your second month, and until you reached the required five days per week for the remaining months of your 8-month goal of learning a musical instrument. You can do the same with the other musical instruments that you have in mind. You need to learn the instrument one at a time to keep your interest.

Do not abandon your goal because it might become a habit and you won't be able to accomplish anything with that. When you try to learn the three instruments at the same time frame and assign a specific schedule for each instrument, it is possible that you might stop learning any of the instruments if you find it more interesting to learn the other instruments. Once you have decided on your goal, you need to see it through and avoid doing things half-heartedly.

You need to consult your doctor first if you have goals that might affect your health, such as losing weight. It is risky to immediately bring down your caloric intakes because such action may damage your muscle tissue, affect your health, and decrease your energy level when you are not supposed to. It is advisable to set small incremental goals in losing weight after consulting your doctor.

Small incremental goals can motivate you a lot. You can see your progress now as you try to meet the original long-term goal.

Chapter 11 - Designing A Plan

To realize your goals that will help you achieve lasting success in your career and personal life, you need to design a plan that will take you there. You need to turn your goals into projects.

It is usually easier to start from your target date of accomplishing the goal. Let us take the example of learning to play a musical instrument. Assuming that today is the 8th month and you can play your chosen musical instrument splendidly. What did you do the month before? You practiced for five days in a week and perhaps some more. What about two months prior? You practiced five days in a week. What about three months prior?

The idea here is to re-trace the steps back to the first step that you took to reach the 8th month with success. It's the same with your other goals. You need to assume that you have already reached your goal and you need to re-trace the steps you need to take in order to arrive at your starting point.

In each step that you have written, you need to analyze if you need to add or delete something in order to make your design more precise and you should eliminate wasted actions. If a certain process is not necessary, then omit it in your design. If you need to add a process within a process to ensure success, then do so.

You can use diagrams, charts, and other forms of visuals to help you with your design. You can include flowcharting, which programmers usually use in creating their computer program. The flowchart can give you an idea as to what goes on with the steps that you intend to take. It can also help you realize the flaw in your process and prompts you to make necessary corrections or modifications.

You need to look at all the angles and include the possible limiting factors and where you need to go or what you need to do in case you encounter an obstacle. You might also need to include other exits in case you need to bail out and start again from your initial stand. Understand that you only need to do such if you really have no way out.

When you design your plan, always look at it as if your life depends on it because it's not far from the truth. You are plotting a way to turn your goals into a reality and to make living more comfortable and easier for you.

Chapter 12 - Carry Out Your Plan And Track Your Progress

You have your goals complete with timeframe and a plan to carry out your goals and make sure to follow your plan to the dot, except when you noticed that you need to make some alterations. It is natural to have holes in your plan especially if this is your initial venture in setting your goals. The important thing at this point is that you have noticed the flaw immediately and you need to patch it up right away.

By now, your journal should be neatly arranged according to priorities (for easy monitoring). You can also have a separate file for the different periods of accomplishing your goal so you can see the ones you have accomplished in each timeframe and the ones that are left. You will also see if a certain goal is not making any progress at all.

You need to keep a regular schedule of monitoring your goals to make certain that everything is moving according to your plan. If you need to add something, just make sure that it is relevant to your goals, other wise you will only introduce chaos in your already systematic plan – you don't want that to happen.

If there is another goal you need to include and it is irrelevant to your current goals, it is best not to include it for now. You can also alter your new goal a little to make it relevant to your current goals, only if it's possible.

Setting your goals must not end with designing a plan to carry out and just wait for your goals to come true. You need to be vigilant and always check that everything is still in proper order.

Chapter 13 - Review Your Goals And See If Something Is Amiss

If for some reason you suddenly realized that a particular goal seems to take too long to accomplish, then there must be something wrong with the goal you set. It is also possible that you need something else to see your goals coming true. You might need to learn a new skill for that particular goal to get accomplished.

Review your goal and see what's missing or perhaps you made a miscalculation. You might need to insert an additional step like learning a new skill or knowledge to accomplish the goal. If the timeframe for that particular goal is not enough to learn the new skill that you need, then you must make necessary adjustments while you still can. Don't delay, because each minute you waste will take you longer in achieving your goal.

Review the remaining goals that you are yet to accomplish and check if you can shorten the timeframe when you incorporate the new skill or knowledge that you have. It is also possible that there are other goals that also require you to learn other skills to make them really work for you.

There are times when you might not be able to see the realization of a certain goal, life sucks sometimes and things happen beyond our control. Not fulfilling a particular goal despite following your plan does not mean you're a loser, it simply tells you that you did not reach the expected result and you need to do better next time.

You can also reward yourself for the goals that you did meet in order to motivate yourself even more.

Set your goals carefully, design a well-made plan, monitor your accomplishments, make necessary adjustments when needed, always be prepared for anything, and you will definitely have better days ahead.

Conclusion

Thank you again for purchasing this book!

I hope this book was able to help you set your goals that will bring you lasting success in your career and personal life.

The next step is to put everything that you have learned into action and enjoy a happy and fulfilled life.

Thank you and good luck!

www.ingramcontent.com/pod-product-compliance
Lightning Source LLC
Chambersburg PA
CBHW070724180526
45167CB00004B/1605